My Name is George

A Collection of Stories about People who Share my Name

By Allison Dearstyne

For Geo the Hero

The name George comes from the ancient Greek word "georgos," which means 'farmer' or 'earth worker.' This comes from the roots *geo,* or 'earth,' and *ergon,* or 'work.' Originally, the name was created to honor Zeus. There is a story in early Greek mythology about Zeus the farmer, or Zeus Georgos, before he became a bigshot among the gods and goddesses. Georgos became the Greek name Georgios, which is translated George in English.

Saint George was the first person to make your name famous in 303 C.E. He was born in modern-day Turkey, and the English claim him as their patron saint. His white flag with a red cross fly over England to this day.

Did you know that there are many famous people who share your name? We will look at these seven remarkable men named George:

George Washington Carver
George Harrison
George Speck
George Herman Ruth, Jr.
George Washington Bush
George Frideric Handel
George Washington

George Washington Carver was a Black American botanist, professor, author, scientist, inventor and man of faith. He was born into slavery sometime in the early 1860s in Missouri. At one week old, he was kidnapped along with his mother and sister, and they were sold as slaves in Kentucky. His master from Missouri hired someone to find them, but only George could be found and was returned to him.

The American Civil War was fought when George was a baby and when it ended in 1865, slavery became illegal. What happened to little George next was quite unusual. His former masters raised him as their own son. They taught him to read and write and encouraged him to continue his education.

He traveled 10 miles away to attend school since he was not allowed to attend his local public school with White children. Young George met a kind woman who helped him by allowing him to live at her house. He introduced himself to her as "Carver's George," the name he had always used, since his master's last name was Carver. What she told him in response stuck with him the rest of his life.

She said, "From now on your name is George Carver. You must learn all you can, then go back out into the world and give your learning back to the people." In his life, he did just that!

George Washington Carver became the first Black student, and later professor, at his college. He earned a reputation as a genius and hard worker. Later, he headed the Agriculture Department at Tuskegee Institute for 47 years. He created a research center and taught methods for effective farming, especially farming peanuts.

George Washington Carver became so famous for teaching about the many uses for peanuts that he became known as the "Peanut Man!" He wrote "How to Grow the Peanut and 105 Ways of Preparing it for Human Consumption." He used peanuts to make all kinds of products, including dyes, plastics and gasoline.

As a teacher, George taught his students to become not only men of intellect, but men of character. Leading by example, he taught them to strive toward these eight virtues:

1. Be clean both inside and out.
2. Neither look up to the rich nor down on the poor.
3. Lose, if need be, without squealing.
4. Win without bragging.
5. Always be considerate of women, children, and older people.
6. Be too brave to lie.
7. Be too generous to cheat.
8. Take your share of the world and let others take theirs.

As a scientist, George gained respect among both Black and White people. He was both a man of science and of faith. Christian faith, he believed, would unite different ethnic groups and end discrimination.

George Washington Carver received many honors during his life and after his death. On his grave is written, "He could have added fortune to fame, but caring for neither, he found happiness and honor in being helpful to the world." You can find happiness and honor in being helpful to the world just like George Washington Carver!

George Harrison was known as "the quiet Beatle." Born in Liverpool, England in 1943, George was the youngest of four children. Later, he was the youngest of the four Beatles, who also considered him a little brother. George remembered his obsession with guitars beginning when he was a young teenager, and how happy he was when his dad bought him his first guitar.

On a school bus he met Paul McCartney, and they formed an instant friendship over their love of music. Paul introduced him to John Lennon, who thought George was a cool kid, but too young to join their band at 15. This proved to be true when the Beatles played in Germany in 1960, and George was kicked out because he was too young to play in nightclubs.

George Harrison became known as "the quiet Beatle" because he was happy to fill the role of the band's talented, but never showy lead guitar player. He began to love Indian culture and introduced Indian instruments into some of the rock 'n roll songs the Beatles wrote. It was a groundbreaking fusion of two different types of music!

The Beatles had their different roles: John Lennon and Paul McCartney wrote songs, Ringo Starr was the drummer, and George Harrison was the lead guitar player. George began songwriting and proved to be good at it! He was frustrated that the other members of his band overlooked his songs when creating albums. A few of his songs are in later Beatles albums, and they became fan favorites. "Something," "Here Comes the Sun," and "While My Guitar Gently Weeps" were all written by George.

After the Beatles split up, people were surprised that quiet George made such successful solo albums. During his solo projects he thought of a wonderful idea to hold a concert to raise funds for charity. In 1971 George recruited some of his famous musician friends to help him raise money for the people in war-torn Bangladesh, which had just been hit by a high flood. A lot of other musicians have followed his example raising money for charity.

George Harrison may have been quiet, but he was still a leader. If you ever feel overlooked, just keep doing your thing and you can be like musical George Harrison!

George Speck was the unlikely inventor of potato chips. He was born in 1824 in Saratoga Lake, New York to parents with Black and American Indian ancestry. When he grew up, he got a job as a cook at an expensive restaurant called Moon's Lake House. Because George was so skilled at cooking and creating recipes, he became the head chef. His sister Kate worked as a cook there too. Once, a customer mistakenly called George Speck "Crum." George joked that a crumb is bigger than a speck and embraced the new nickname.

One evening while cooking dinner, Kate was making french fries for a customer. The customer complained that they were too thick, so he kept sending them back to the kitchen to be remade. George was not happy that someone complained about the food. To get revenge, George prepared one more batch of potatoes, but this time he sliced them super thin. He fried them in oil, the same as the french fries, which made the potatoes dark and crisp. Determined to insult the customer, George added salt, put them on a plate and served them. But when the customer tried the thin crispy fries, he absolutely loved them!

From that point on George began preparing potatoes in this manner and they became known as "Saratoga Chips." George's chips became so popular that people would come from all over just to get a taste! The owner of the restaurant tried to take credit for creating the chips by producing and selling them in boxes with his name on them. Unfortunately, George never patented the potato chip, so he never got credit for the invention. There is even speculation that the whole idea was his sister's.

In 1860 George opened his own restaurant in Saratoga Lake. He named it Crum's House, and he put potato chips as appetizers on every table! The restaurant was successful and operated for 30 years. George never sold his chips outside of his restaurant.

Now potato chips are sold all over the world! Every time you eat a potato chip, think about George Speck's success when he was just trying to teach a picky customer a lesson!

George Herman Ruth, Jr. earned so many nicknames for his outstanding baseball career, it's hard to keep track of them all! If you ever hear someone talking about "The Sultan of Swat," "The Bambino," "The Babe," "Home Run King," or his most famous one, "Babe Ruth," they are taking about George Herman Ruth, Jr. In 1895 he was born very close to present-day Orioles Park in Maryland.

He was a mischievous little boy and when he was seven, his parents sent him to a Catholic reformatory school to straighten him out. At his school, little George was described as "incorrigible." That means his behavior was so bad, his teachers didn't think he would ever improve. A school disciplinarian taught him to play baseball as an outlet, and mischievous little George grew up to be the world's best baseball player!

He first played minor-league baseball for the Baltimore Orioles in 1914, but his contract was sold to the Red Sox after less than a year. George helped them win the World Series three times as the pitcher, but he wanted to hit too. On some baseball teams like the Red Sox, the pitcher doesn't go to bat. So, he switched positions to be an outfielder. It didn't take long for him to break the Major League Baseball single-season home run record in 1919!

After his stellar season, the Red Sox owner sold George's contract to the Yankees, and Yankee fans were thrilled! The Red Sox fans weren't so happy, though. Their team didn't win the World Series for another 86 years, and fans called this fateful decision "The Curse of the Bambino." George played for the Yankees for 15 years and helped them win four World Series championships. He broke all kinds of records playing for the Yankees, and some of them stand today. His greatest achievement was hitting 60 home runs in one season!

During his years as a baseball star, George liked to visit children in hospitals and orphanages. His fans loved him, and he became a symbol for the United States long after he stopped playing baseball. He was legendary!

If you struggle to be well-behaved, then you are in good company with Babe Ruth. Try baseball as an outlet! You never know, it could change your life like it changed life for George Herman Ruth, Jr!

George Washington Bush was a Black American pioneer who shaped Washington state's early history. He was born in Pennsylvania in 1789, the only child of his African father and Irish mother. When he grew up, he moved west and became a cattle rancher and fur trapper. George was one of the best fur trappers in Missouri and saved the small fortune he earned.

In 1830 he married a nurse named Isabella James, and together they had nine sons. The Bushes decided to make a big move further west on the Oregon Trail. Back in those days, most of the people who lived in the Pacific Northwest were American Indians. Very few others made the dangerous journey. The Oregon Trail was over 2,000 miles long, and groups traveled together in covered wagons. George and Isabella bought covered wagons for five other families to make the journey with them.

The Bush family history records that George built a false bottom into his covered wagon to hide silver and gold. Their original plan was to settle in present-day Oregon, but a new law did not allow Black people to own land there. So, the Bushes and their friends settled in present-day Washington in a territory that both the United States and Great Britain claimed.

The families built a sawmill, a logging company and a farm. The Bushes built a hotel where anyone could stay for free. Weary travelers were given a meal and some crops. The Bushes helped their American Indian neighbors through outbreaks of smallpox and measles. If a neighbor had a bad year with crops, the Bushes always shared happily, rather than selling their crops for a lot of money.

Some historians say that George Washington Bush's generosity helped many Americans settle in Washington, which populated the territory. This helped settle the land dispute in favor of the United States. His influence in the Pacific Northwest was tremendous!

The Bushes were probably everyone's favorite neighbors. Whenever you have a chance to show kindness to your neighbors, take it and think about generous George Washington Bush!

George Frideric Handel was a composer whose music you often hear around Christmastime. Born in Halle, Germany in 1685, George loved music right from the start. His strict father didn't think that he could realistically make a career in music, and he didn't allow George to take music lessons or even own an instrument. But George's mother, seeing her son's talent and love for music, allowed him to practice in secret.

Once, little George had an opportunity to play the organ in front of a duke. When he played, others noticed his extraordinary talent and suggested to his father that he be given music lessons. His father finally agreed, and over the next few years George learned how to play many instruments, and his favorite was the oboe. When he was nine, he began composing music, which means he created music in his head and then wrote it out on paper.

After four years in lessons George became more talented than his tutor! Despite George's dedication to music, his father insisted that he study law instead. In law school, several Lutheran professors influenced him to be generous with the wealth he would one day gain. George did well in law school, but dropped out because law wasn't his passion. Instead, he continued composing music.

George had a successful career in Italy, then he moved to England, where he lived the rest of his life. There, he composed a piece for the coronation, or ceremony where the king is crowned. That piece, called "Zadok the Priest" has been played at every coronation since, and is considered a British patriotic anthem.

His most famous composition is "Messiah," which contains passages from the Bible. The most well-known part of "Messiah" is the "Hallelujah Chorus." At the end of his composition Handel wrote the letters "SDG", short for Soli Deo Gloria, a Latin phrase which is translated, "To God alone the Glory."

George believed his talent came from God, for the purpose of serving God. The next time you hear the "Hallelujah Chorus," sing along and think about talented George Frideric Handel!

George Washington is called the "Father of the Country" for his irreplaceable role in shaping the United States. He was born in 1732 in the British colony of Virginia. When George was 11 his father died, and he had to drop out of school so that he could work on his family's farm. Although his formal education ended, he continued to learn all he could informally.

As a teenager, he mostly learned outdoors, especially farming and surveying land. At 16, he took the initiative to travel with a group of surveyors to improve his skills in plotting land. For a few years, he made a career out of surveying land, which made him tough and resourceful. He bought and inherited some land as a young man, including his beloved Mount Vernon home.

In 1754 a war began in the colonies between Britain and France because both countries claimed the same territory. George jumped at the opportunity to serve in the British military. He made some huge mistakes during the war, and humbled, he chose to learn from them. After the British won the war, he married a widow named Martha Custis and helped her raise her two children.

Not long after the war, George began to disagree with some laws the British made for the colonies. He encouraged others to stop buying British goods until they made some changes. Eventually the colonists wanted independence from Britain.

When the American Revolution began, George showed up ready to fight. Troops rallied behind him as their commander, and he led them through hard times when it seemed they would surely be defeated. With help from France, George led the troops to an unexpected victory for the United States.

After the war, George Washington considered his job done and went back to Mount Vernon. For four years, the young country struggled under a weak government. This led to division between the states, and serious problems for the national government. It became clear to George that his country needed him again, this time to help fix the problems in the government.

In the summer of 1787 George and other leaders went to Philadelphia and got to work. They decided to scrap the weak government and create a brand-new one. It was a hard job because they disagreed about almost everything! By the end of the summer, they had drafted the United States Constitution as the new form of government. The writers wisely made a way for future laws to be written so the Constitution could change over time.

Everyone voted for George Washington to be the first president. He didn't even want the job, but again he rose to the occasion to serve his country. George set many good examples that future presidents followed. Instead of being addressed with a fancy royal title, he simply wanted to be called "Mr. President." He surrounded himself with smart people to advise him. Four years later, he was elected to serve a second term. Four years after that, people wanted to elect him a third time, but George said no. He didn't think it was good for one person to have so much power. Almost every president since has followed his example.

It's hard to imagine what the United States would be without George Washington. The next time you look at the portrait on a one-dollar bill or quarter, be inspired by the story of the "Father of the Country," George Washington!

This page is all about you!

_____ was born on

_____

As a baby, George _____

_____

As a little boy, George _____

_____

George is especially good at _____

_____

George is often described as _____

_____

George makes people laugh when he _____

_____

One day George would like to _____

_____

This page is for making a self-portrait. A self-portrait is a picture of you, drawn by you!

Bibliography

Biography.com editors. "George Washington Carver Biography." *The Biography.com website.* A&E Television Networks, 27 Apr. 2017. Web. 21 Jul. 2018.

Biography.com editors. "George Frideric Handel Biography." *The Biography.com website.* A&E Television Networks, 27 May 2021. Web. 22 Jun. 2021.

Biography.com editors. "George Harrison Biography." *The Biography.com website.* A&E Television Networks, 20 Apr. 2021. Web. 18 May. 2021.

Biography.com editors. "Babe Ruth Biography." *The Biography.com website.* A&E Television Networks, 7 Apr. 2021. Web. 28 May 2021.

BlackInventor.com editors. "George Crum: Inventor of Potato Chips." *BlackInventors.com.* Famous Black Inventors: A Rich Heritage Gives Way to Modern Ingenuity. Web. 09 Jan. 2019.

Collins, Michael. "Saint George." Britannia History. *The Britannia.com website.* Web. 21 Jul. 2018.

Wikipedia contributors. "George (given name)." *Wikipedia, The Free Encyclopedia.* Wikipedia, The Free Encyclopedia, 13 Jul. 2018. Web. 28 Jul. 2018

Wikipedia contributors. "George Washington Bush." *Wikipedia, The Free Encyclopedia*. Wikipedia, The Free Encyclopedia, 14 Nov. 2019. Web. 1 Dec. 2019.

Wikipedia contributors. "George Washington Carver." *Wikipedia, The Free Encyclopedia*. Wikipedia, The Free Encyclopedia, 19 Jul. 2018. Web. 21 Jul. 2018.

Wikipedia contributors. "George Crum." *Wikipedia, The Free Encyclopedia*. Wikipedia, The Free Encyclopedia, 9 Jan. 2019. Web. 9 Jan. 2019.

Wikipedia contributors. "George Frideric Handel." *Wikipedia, The Free Encyclopedia*. Wikipedia, The Free Encyclopedia, 3 Jul. 2018. Web. 21 Jul. 2018.

Wikipedia contributors. "George Harrison." *Wikipedia, The Free Encyclopedia*. Wikipedia, The Free Encyclopedia, 20 Jul. 2018 Web. 21 Jul. 2018

Wikipedia contributors. "George Washington." *Wikipedia, The Free Encyclopedia*. Wikipedia, The Free Encyclopedia, 21 Jul. 2018. Web. 21 Jul. 2018

www.ingramcontent.com/pod-product-compliance
Lightning Source LLC
Chambersburg PA
CBHW042111040426
42448CB00002B/222